Ta

Harness the Magickal Power of the Tarot

Copyright Information

Copyright © 2015 by Kadmon, Baal

All rights reserved. No part of this book may be reproduced by any mechanical, photographic, or electrical process, or in the form of a recording. Nor may it be stored in a storage/retrieval system nor transmitted or otherwise be copied for private or public use-other than "fair use" as quotations in articles or reviews—without the prior written consent of the Author.

The Information in this book is solely for educational purposes and not for the treatment, diagnosis or prescription of any diseases. This text is not meant to provide financial or health advice of any sort. The Author and the publisher are in no way liable for any use or misuse of the material. No Guarantee of results is being made in this text.

Kadmon, Baal
Tarot Magick – Harness the Magickal Power of the Tarot

–1st ed

Printed in the United States of America

Cover image: #53203854 Author l.Ivan Fotolia.com

Images of the individual Tarot cards are in the public domain in the United States Where this book is published. Please reference https://en.wikipedia.org. Under each card I will provide a link to the Wikipedia page for reference.

Book Cover Design: Baal Kadmon

At the best of our ability we have credited those who created the pictures based on the research we have conducted. If there are images in the book that have not been given due copyright notice please contact us at Resheph@baalkadmon.com and we will remedy the situation by giving proper copyright credit or we will remove the image/s at your request.

Disclaimer

Disclaimer: By law, I need to add this statement.
This book is for educational purposes only and does not claim to prevent or cure any disease. The advice and methods in this book should not be construed as financial, medical or psychological treatment. Please seek advice from a professional if you have serious financial, medical or psychological issues.
By purchasing, reading and or listening to this book, you understand that results are not guaranteed. In light of this, you understand that in the event that this book or audio does not work or causes harm in any area of your life, you agree that you do not hold Baal Kadmon, Amazon, its employees or affiliates liable for any damages you may experience or incur.
The Text and or Audio in this series are copyrighted 2015

Introduction

Occultism and magick is rife with symbols. In fact, the very basis of magick and occult is symbology. Everything is symbolic of some higher truth. From the rituals we preform to the books we read. We are immersed in the power and magick of symbols. Although I am of the school of thought that symbols are not 100% necessary so long as you have a strong inner intention and can control your mind during a ritual, I use them nonetheless. In my rituals, if you have read my other books are paired-down. They have symbols but do not overrun you with complicated devices. However, there are moments in the occultists and magicians life that require us to pay attention to symbols. Often these symbols can give you insight into your life. The tarot cards are one aspect of occultism that I feel is worth paying close attention to. The symbols that is.

Tarot cards have been used for centuries, some say even thousands of years to either foretell the future or to give the person who is having the reading a sense of direction towards life in general or for a very specific issue they are having. I have had my tarot cards read several times and I always found them insightful. Yes, it is helpful if the person who is reading the tarot cards for you is knowledgeable, but often the symbols themselves, if you pay close attention can give you some guidance. Since you do not have control over the cards you draw; the shuffling and choosing of cards becomes an unconscious act. Something, a spirit perhaps or just your subconscious mind is guiding your hands to pick the cards that you pick. Some would say even fate herself.

In this book, we will not be focusing on tarot cards as a source of knowledge about the future, there are plenty of good books about that. We will be dealing with the tarot cards in a different way, we will be using them as a driving force for magickal practice. It is a fair assessment to say that Tarot card symbology is quite powerful and aside from divination it can be driving engine for magick. I know personally, I used it. I used to get someone back into my life. It worked so well that I needed to have the ritual reversed by a powerful Shaman. So please take heed, tarot cards are a very powerful magnet. Their symbols have a spiritual force. In the next chapter, we will discuss, ever so briefly, the reason why symbols are so powerful and how why they are much more than just contrived ideas of the mind, then we will discuss the tarot in general and then to the rituals. Let us being.

The Importance of Symbols

We often look at cultures outside of our spheres to be somewhat alien. You must admit, when you step off a plane into a foreign country that has almost nothing in common with where you come from, it causes your mind to go into an instant of "Wow, this is weird". It's not because we are ignorant or that we lack the open minded to embrace other cultures, it is just that we are so different that it often strikes us odd when we see something so different from our own. It's almost automatic, it's unconscious. And it's natural. BUT, if you look closer, under all the customs and mores, you find elements within world cultures and religious systems that are strikingly the same. If you look back into religious history you will find the cross very prominent. At the dawn of humanity, way before Christianity, the cross had a significance not unlike the Christian conception. It was considered a symbol of the sun, (no coincidence that Jesus is often equated with the Sun God?). In Ancient Egypt, the cross is a symbol of life in the form of the "Ankh". The Christian cross, although the object on which Jesus died, represents LIFE. It's through Jesus suffering and death on the cross that we are saved, that is according to the Christian understanding. That is of course, one of many symbols I can choose from. Aside from those basic symbols like the cross, the circle and the triangle which all cultures share. There is a deeper level of symbology that involves certain essences of an individual. Such as the warrior, the magician, the Goddess, the fool. As well as certain motifs such as the dying and resurrecting God, Osiris, Shamash, Jesus, Mithra to name just a very few. There seems to be some commonality despite the apparently disparate nature of world culture.

If you look at the stories of mythology and even modern day religious texts, you will find, motifs such as the warrior, the virgin, Immaculate Conception, star crossed lovers, the witch, the warlock, the judge. The stories have the same motifs, they are just garbed in different clothing. There is clearly a universal connection here. Those symbols mean something, if they didn't, they would not be following us back to the dawn of humanity. Even many of our creation narratives start in very much the same way and have very similar motifs. We will not go into those here, but if you would like a good book on parallel creation myths please read " Parallel Myths by J.F. Bierlein", Its very interesting.

Much of why we share so much of our narratives may remain a mystery, but Carl Jung, a Swedish psychologist came up with by far, the most persuasive answer, at least as far as I am concerned. He came up with the idea of the "collective unconscious" and the concept of the "archetypes".

What Are Archetypes?

They are in many ways the structure of the collective unconscious (which I will get into shortly). They are innate tendencies that reflect our common humanity. Motifs like I mentioned above are all common themes. These commonalities flow through all our spiritual traditions. They often manifest in something called "Archetypal images" within religious texts, dreams and spiritual visions. Essentially many of the characters in mythology and their stories are archetypal in nature. This also applies to all the biblical motifs and individuals as well. Whether the people in the bible existed or not is not the purpose of this book, but no matter what their historical status maybe, they represent archetypical behaviors and demeanors. The hero and the villain are perfect examples of the archetypal form. It might sound odd that I would be writing this in a book on Tarot magick, but the tarot is pretty much a deck of cards with all the archetypical symbols on them. So I feel that it is always good to know some background as to why the tarot are so powerful. However, before we go into the actual tarot themselves, let me quickly give you an overview of the collective unconscious. All this will give you a better perspective as to why the Tarot is what it is and why it is so powerful.

What is the Collective Unconscious?

It is the very backbone of our mind. We are all born with it and did not learn any of it. Rather, this part of the mind is innate. You can call it a kind of universal library of human experience and knowledge. Spiritual experiences, according to Jung, must emerge from the collective unconscious via archetypical forms.

Jung said it best " *the collective unconscious - so far as we can say anything about it at all - appears to consist of mythological motifs or primordial images, for which reason the myths of all nations are its real exponents. In fact, the whole of mythology could be taken as a sort of projection of the collective unconscious... We can therefore study the collective unconscious in two ways, either in mythology or in the analysis of the individual.* (From The Structure of the Psyche, CW 8, par. 325.)."

It is with that that we will proceed to the Tarot, a deck of cards infused with mythological motifs and primordial images.

The Tarot Cards

(What follows is a very cursory history, we will be more concerned about their magickal qualities.)

If you have read anything about the tarot you will have probably read it might be traced back to the ancient Egyptians or to hermetic traditions. This may or may not be true; I wouldn't be surprised if it is.

The only problem is, is that we do not have proof of this. We do, however, have more proof that the tarot cards came from more modern times. This does not detract from their powers since they are still in possession of primordial and archetypal imagery. The tarot decks as we know them today were first seen in Italy around the 1400s. It was not clear if they were used initially for gambling or just as a card game of sorts. However, it was soon made into an oracle and came to be classified into the occult science of cartomancy. Cartomancy is the use of cards for fortune telling purposes. There are various methods of cartomancy. You can even use a normal deck of card, the kind you play poker with. However, the tarot is a bit different. Tarot became so popular it was soon condemned as an instrument of the devil. This was made possible because the bible specifically forbids any form of fortunetelling.

A tarot deck is comprised of two suits of cards; the Major Arcana and Minor arcana. This classification was coined by the writer Ellic Howe. We will be mostly focused on the Major Arcana in this book.

The Major Arcana: Is a suit of 22 cards. These 22 cards represent deep archetypes of the collective unconscious as I stated earlier. In fact, a Jungian analyst by the name of Salie Nichols wrote about them and stated that they contain deep archetypical and psychological significance to the individual. He went so far as to say that the cards themselves are the key to a person's full potential or as he put it " The Entire individuation process"… In essence, a key to the total transformation of the psyche.

The 22 cards are as follows:

The fool

The Magician

The High Priestess

The Empress

The Emperor

The Hierophant

The Lovers

The chariot

Strength

The Hermit

Wheel of fortune

Justice

The Hanged Man

Death

Temperance

The Devil

The Tower

The Stars

The Moon

The Sun

Judgment

The World

We will discuss the significance of each one in the next chapter.

The Minor Arcana: Since we will not be dealing much with the minor arcana, I won't go into great depth about them. However, I feel it is good to know at least some cursory knowledge about them. These are the second suite of cards in a typical tarot deck. There are 56 in number and are divided into 4 sub suits. Cups, swords, coins and wands. Not unlike the spades, hearts, diamonds and clubs found in conventional playing decks. They are meant to be lesser cards. As opposed to the major arcana, the minor arcana are thought to represent the more mundane aspects of life. Such as:

Swords: General reason

Wands: Creativity and will

Coins: Material body and material possessions.

Cups: Emotions and love.

Now I would like to make clear when I say more mundane aspects I am not saying unimportant. What I am saying is that the major arcana represent more spiritual and lofty aspects of the human condition, whereas the minor arcana do not. Although we will not be using the minor arcana, there is nothing stopping you from using them in your magick as well. All you will need to ascertain their respective meanings is a good book that defines each one. I highly recommend "The Easiest Way to Learn the Tarot – Ever!! – By Dusty White" for this purpose. In the next chapter, we will go into a bit more depth regarding the major arcana since we will be using them for our rituals.

The Major Arcana

We will now discuss the major arcana and the meaning and powers behind them, as well as their ritual purpose.

https://en.wikipedia.org/wiki/File:RWS_Tarot_00_Fool.jpg

The Fool: *This card is a metaphor for ones journey through life. It is a card of new beginnings. It is called the Fool, not so much to indicate foolishness but rather of innocence and faith. We will use this card in our ritual for new beginnings.*

https://en.wikipedia.org/wiki/File:RWS_Tarot_01_Magician.jpg

The Magician: *The Magician is a very powerful and positive card. It represents the active and creative impulses in man. It is through the magician that we exert our power in this world. We will use this card to create change in your lives.*

https://en.wikipedia.org/wiki/File:RWS_Tarot_02_High_Priestess.jpg

The High Priestess: *This card is also quite powerful and represents, like the magician our creative impulse; however, it is more latent and passive. She represents all we can be. We will use this card to become conscious of our life purpose.*

https://en.wikipedia.org/wiki/File:RWS_Tarot_03_Empress.jpg

The Empress: *This card is motherly card and represents nature and its abundance. We will use this card to connect to abundance.*

https://en.wikipedia.org/wiki/File:RWS_Tarot_04_Emperor.jpg

The Emperor: *This card represents rules, structure and discipline. We will use this card to gain stability in our lives.*

https://en.wikipedia.org/wiki/File:RWS_Tarot_05_Hierophant.jpg

The Hierophant: *This card represents esoteric knowledge and mysteries. We will use this card to acquire hidden and spiritual knowledge.*

https://en.wikipedia.org/wiki/File:RWS_Tarot_06_Lovers.jpg

The Lovers: *This card expresses both love and sexuality. It represents the union of a couple. We will use this card to help us get into a loving relationship.*

https://en.wikipedia.org/wiki/File:RWS_Tarot_07_Chariot.jpg

The Chariot: *This card is one of assertiveness and confidence. It represents stability and ambition as well. We will use this card for our ritual on Self-confidence.*

https://en.wikipedia.org/wiki/File:RWS_Tarot_08_Strength.jpg

Strength: *This card represents strength, tolerance, perseverance and patience. We will use this card to gain strength in the face of adversity.*

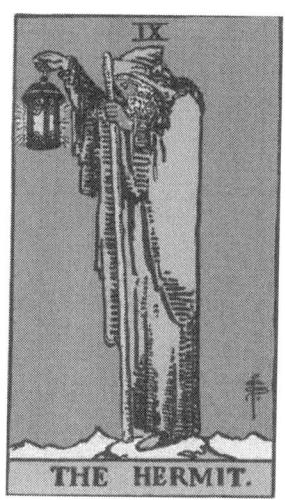

https://en.wikipedia.org/wiki/File:RWS_Tarot_09_Hermit.jpg

The Hermit: *This card is about soul searching and finding out who you really are. We will be using this card to connect with our inward life and become more mindful.*

https://en.wikipedia.org/wiki/File:RWS_Tarot_10_Wheel_of_Fortune.jpg

Wheel of Fortune: *This is the card of connections. How the universe works and all the intricate connections that make it work. We will use this card to see the bigger picture and see the divine lining inherit in it.*

https://en.wikipedia.org/wiki/File:RWS_Tarot_11_Justice.jpg

Justice: *This card is about accountability to ones actions as well as decisiveness. We will use this card to gain clarity on an issue or issues.*

https://en.wikipedia.org/wiki/File:RWS_Tarot_12_Hanged_Man.jpg

The Hanged Man: *This is the card of letting go. Much like the Strength card, it teaches patience and tolerance. We will use this to help us let go of a trauma or other kind of hurt.*

https://en.wikipedia.org/wiki/File:RWS_Tarot_13_Death.jpg

Death: *This card is about letting go of baggage that does not serve us anymore. It's a card of changer. We will use it to break away from the past and move forward into the future without fear.*

https://en.wikipedia.org/wiki/File:RWS_Tarot_14_Temperance.jpg

Temperance: This card is about living in harmony within oneself. This is the card of integration and thus we will use this card to bring our disparate parts together so we can become whole.

https://en.wikipedia.org/wiki/File:RWS_Tarot_15_Devil.jpg

The Devil: *This card represents our tendency to be bound by our emotions and the material world. It represents ignorance of the truth and hopelessness in life itself. We will use this card to help us break the bondage that we are in. It could also be a person you might think is keeping you in an emotional prison.*

https://en.wikipedia.org/wiki/File:RWS_Tarot_16_Tower.jpg

The Tower: *This card represents the crumbling of the ego identity. Often we are too proud and or aloof to see how ego driven we are. With this card, we will destroy the contorted lens of the ego so you can see the truth of things.*

https://en.wikipedia.org/wiki/File:RWS_Tarot_17_Star.jpg

The Stars: *This card is about hope, serenity and inspiration. This is a card about faith. We will use it to help you gain faith and hope about something in your life.*

https://en.wikipedia.org/wiki/File:RWS_Tarot_18_Moon.jpg

The Moon: *This card is one of active imagination, magick and mystery. We will use this card to help us open our minds to mystery and enhance our power as a magician.*

https://en.wikipedia.org/wiki/File:RWS_Tarot_19_Sun.jpg

The Sun: *This card symbolizes enlightenment and lucidity, vitality and personal greatness. We will use this card to become the best versions of ourselves so we can be successful in all that we do.*

https://en.wikipedia.org/wiki/File:RWS_Tarot_20_Judgement.jpg

Judgment: *This is a card of transformation. It's a card of joy and courage. We will use this card to bring joy into your lives and a sense of purpose.*

https://en.wikipedia.org/wiki/File:RWS_Tarot_21_World.jpg

The World: *This symbolizes the end goal; the ultimate in individuation and accomplishment. This card represents steadfastness and security. We will use this card as an overriding one for general success and fulfillment.*

As you can see, the cards can be very useful for deep inner work. Unlike the other magick books, we will not be focusing on controlling your enemies or to control the weather etc. Let us know discuss what you will need to make these rituals work better for you. After that, we will jump into the rituals themselves.

Tools of Tarot Magick

Although I am not that big on magickal props, I do realize that, at times, one needs them to focus their energies. While only the Tarot cards are mandatory, I do suggest these items below to help you maintain focus.

1. **Tarot cards**: I have several Tarot card decks, many I have because of their beautiful artwork. Here are a few that I recommend.

   The Original Rider Waite Tarot Pack

   The Hermetic Tarot

   The Witches Tarot

2. **Incense:** Frankincense and Myrrh incense. This is a beautifully sacred fragrance and I use it in almost all my rituals, across all forms of magick that I practice.

3. **Candles**: Like in most rituals, there are candles involved. Here are a few you will need. I used to get them individually but I found an amazing source that sells 10 candle colors, 4 of each for a total of 40 candles for an excellent price. I just discovered them and will use them from now on. The colors are red, pink, orange, yellow, green, blue, purple, black, white and violet. "Spell Candles (40 candles)" I will indicate the colors below and their meanings.

   Red: This candle is for love and personal power.

   Pink: Faith, devotion and tenderness.

Orange: For energy, success, cleanses negativity, creates motivation.

Yellow: Confidence, power, knowledge and healing.

Green: Nature and connection to nature. Attracts bodily healing and promotes growth in all ways.

Blue: Spirituality, Harmony at oneness and divinity.

Purple: Success, the attainment of all desires. Psychic powers and the acquisition of mystery knowledge.

Black: Change, protection, black magick, to banish negativity of all sorts be it mental or spiritual in nature.

White: Purity, higher consciousness, peace, truth and unity.

Violet: High levels of spiritual attainment and power. Will help increase magickal ability.

That is all you will need. You will see that these rituals are so easy you will think they are too good to be true. Magick does not have to be difficult for it to work. I think its time to change that old paradigm once and for all. In the next chapter we will go through the 22 rituals. Won't you join me?

22 Tarot Rituals

To perform a simple Tarot Card ritual is very easy. I will go through the steps below. Please note, you may perform these rituals at any time. In this case, you do not need to wait for specific days to arrive. The Tarot cards themselves have a self-possessed power and do not rely on astrological forces, although taking them into account will not impede your outcome. .

1. Place the main tarot card at the center. For example, if we are using the fool card as the main driver for the ritual you would put it in the center of your altar.
2. Pick up the main card and think about the intention you have for this ritual.
3. Say the prayer to the spiritual guardians of the tarot. You may use your wording, this is just an example that I use.
4. Place the main card back in its place.
5. From the same deck, randomly pull out 5 cards. Place those cards in such a way that they encircle the main card. As seen below.
6. Place the candle right before the 1st card. As seen below. You can light and place the incense wherever you like. The incense is more for the ambience.
7. Visualize a white light coming and encircling the main card.

8. Sit in silence and think about your intended outcome.
9. Take out a tarot card book and read the descriptions of the 5 cards that are encircling the main card. Does it give you any insight into your issue?
10. Thank the spiritual guardians of the tarot and release them.
11. For the next 10 days, carry the main card with you wherever you go. Place it under your pillow at night. Every time you touch it, think of your intention.

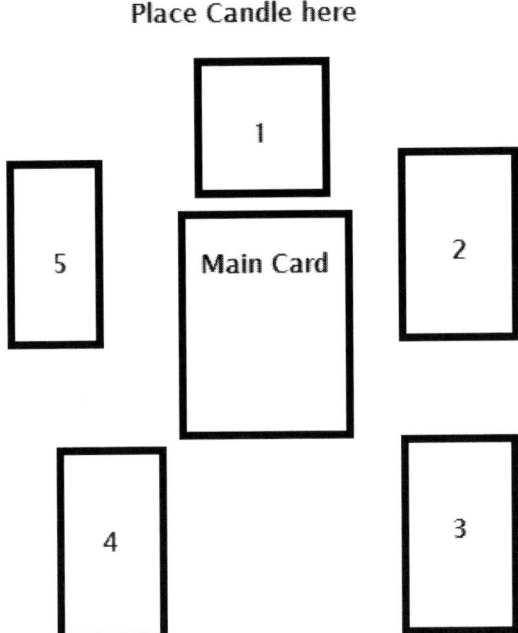

That concludes the ritual. I will be sure to itemize these instructions for each of the 22 rituals below. This way you will have it readily available. The steps will be tailored to the ritual. You see? Not very difficult is it? Do not believe those who would have you do elaborate rituals that require you to do things that are burdensome. Magick is natural and should come as naturally to you as drinking water. Elaborate rituals only serve the egoic tendency for structure and do nothing to contribute to the actual magick itself. In fact, in a future volume I will discuss why magick works at all. Stay tuned…With that said, let us proceed to the rituals.

RITUAL 1 – THE FOOL: A RITUAL FOR NEW BEGINNINGS

1. Place **the fool card** at the center of the altar.
2. Pick up the card and think about the intention you have for this ritual.
3. Say the prayer to the spiritual guardians of the tarot. You may use your wording, this is just an example that I use.

   "Hear me Oh Great Guardians of the Tarot, harness me the power of this great card that I may start my life anew, may this card be the presentation of all things good and new. So Mote it me."
4. Place the card back in its spot.
5. From the same deck, randomly pull out 5 cards. Place those cards in such a way that they encircle the main card. As seen below.

6. Place the **Yellow** candle right before the 1st card. As seen below. You can light and place the incense wherever you like. The incense is more for the ambience.
7. Visualize a white light coming and encircling the main card.
8. Sit in silence and think about your intended outcome.
9. Take out a tarot card book and read the descriptions of the 5 cards that are encircling the main card. Does it give you any insight into your issue?
10. Thank the spiritual guardians of the tarot and release them.
11. For the next 10 days, carry the **fool** card with you wherever you go. Place it under your pillow at night. Every time you touch it, think of your intention.

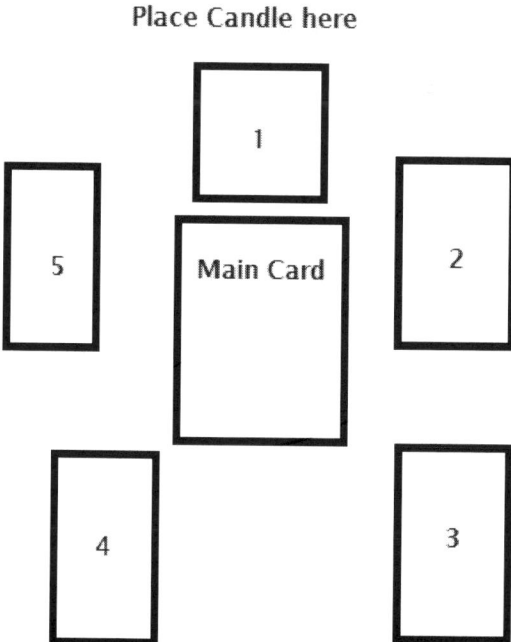

That concludes the ritual.

RITUAL 2 – THE MAGICIAN: A RITUAL FOR BRINING ABOUT CHANGE.

1. Place **the Magician card** at the center of the altar.
2. Pick up the card and think about the intention you have for this ritual.
3. Say the prayer to the spiritual guardians of the tarot. You may use your wording, this is just an example that I use.

   "Hear me Oh Great Guardians of the Tarot, harness me the power of this great and holy card that I may bring forth positive change into my life, may this card be the presentation of all change that is for my good and for the good of all. So Mote it me."
4. Place the card back in its spot.

5. From the same deck, randomly pull out 5 cards. Place those cards in such a way that they encircle the main card. As seen below.
6. Place the **black** candle right before the 1st card. As seen below. You can light and place the incense wherever you like. The incense is more for the ambience.
7. Visualize a white light coming and encircling the main card.
8. Sit in silence and think about your intended outcome.
9. Take out a tarot card book and read the descriptions of the 5 cards that are encircling the main card. Does it give you any insight into your issue?
10. Thank the spiritual guardians of the tarot and release them.
11. For the next 10 days, carry the **magician** card with you wherever you go. Place it under your pillow at night. Every time you touch it, think of your intention.

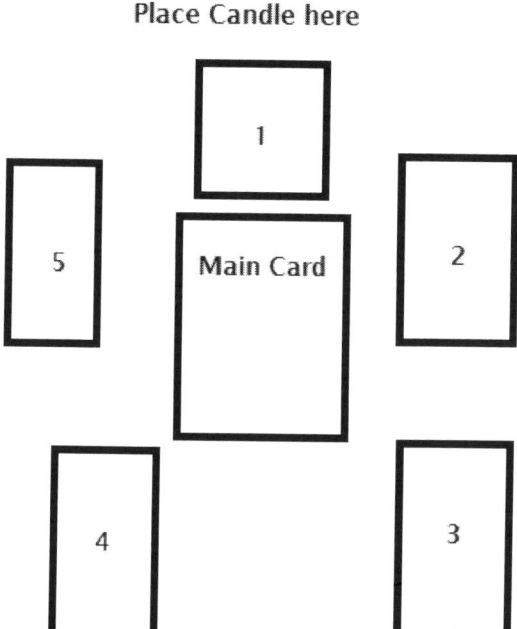

That concludes the ritual.

RITUAL 3 – THE HIGH PRIESTESS: A RITUAL TO FIND YOUR LIFE PURPOSE

1. Place **the High Priestess card** at the center of the altar.
2. Pick up the card and think about the intention you have for this ritual.
3. Say the prayer to the spiritual guardians of the tarot. You may use your wording, this is just an example that I use.

   "Hear me Oh Great Guardians of the Tarot, harness me the power of this holy card that I may find my intended and divine purpose. May this card attract to me the my divine calling. So Mote it me."
4. Place the card back in its spot.
5. From the same deck, randomly pull out 5 cards. Place those cards in such a way that they encircle the main card. As seen below.

6. Place the **orange** candle right before the 1st card. As seen below. You can light and place the incense wherever you like. The incense is more for the ambience.
7. Visualize a white light coming and encircling the main card.
8. Sit in silence and think about your intended outcome.
9. Take out a tarot card book and read the descriptions of the 5 cards that are encircling the main card. Does it give you any insight into your issue?
10. Thank the spiritual guardians of the tarot and release them.
11. For the next 10 days, carry the **High Priestess** card with you wherever you go. Place it under your pillow at night. Every time you touch it, think of your intention.

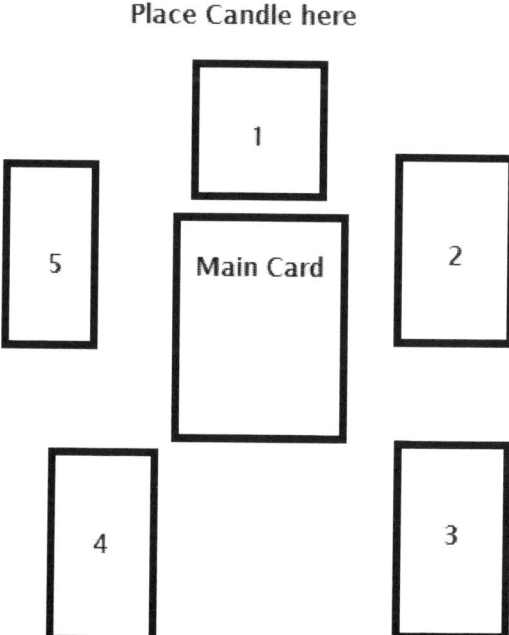

That concludes the ritual.

RITUAL 4 – THE EMPRESS: A RITUAL TO ATTRACT ABUNDANCE

1. Place **the Empress card** at the center of the altar.
2. Pick up the card and think about the intention you have for this ritual.
3. Say the prayer to the spiritual guardians of the tarot. You may use your wording, this is just an example that I use.

   "Hear me Oh Great Guardians of the Tarot, harness me the power of this card, the card of manifestation that I may be blessed and bestowed with material abundance for the good of all. May this card attract to me abundance now. So Mote it me."
4. Place the card back in its spot.

5. From the same deck, randomly pull out 5 cards. Place those cards in such a way that they encircle the main card. As seen below.
6. Place the **orange and yellow** candle right before the 1st card. As seen below. You can light and place the incense wherever you like. The incense is more for the ambience.
7. Visualize a white light coming and encircling the main card.
8. Sit in silence and think about your intended outcome.
9. Take out a tarot card book and read the descriptions of the 5 cards that are encircling the main card. Does it give you any insight into your issue?
10. Thank the spiritual guardians of the tarot and release them.
11. For the next 10 days, carry the **Empress** card with you wherever you go. Place it under your pillow at night. Every time you touch it, think of your intention.

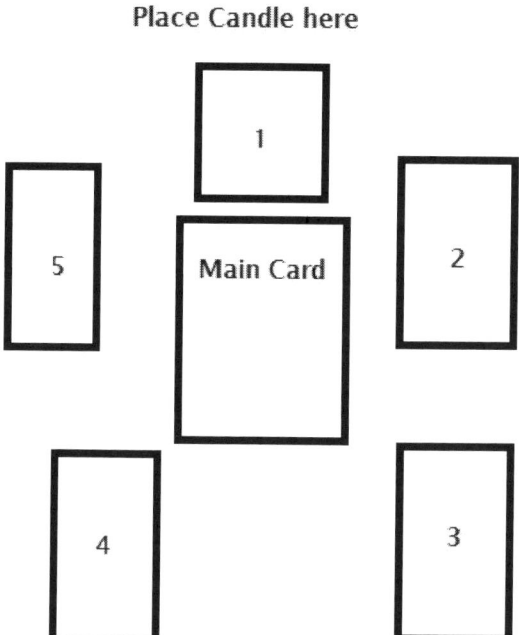

That concludes the ritual.

RITUAL 5 – THE EMPEROR: A RITUAL TO GAIN STABILITY IN LIFE

1. Place **the Emperor card** at the center of the altar.
2. Pick up the card and think about the intention you have for this ritual.
3. Say the prayer to the spiritual guardians of the tarot. You may use your wording, this is just an example that I use.
   "Hear me Oh Great Guardians of the Tarot, harness me the power of this card, the card of strength and inner stability. Hear me so that I may be blessed and bestowed with peace and stability in all my endeavors. So Mote it me."
4. Place the card back in its spot.
5. From the same deck, randomly pull out 5 cards. Place those cards in such a way that they encircle the main card. As seen below.

6. Place the **red and purple** candles right before the 1st card. As seen below. You can light and place the incense wherever you like. The incense is more for the ambience.
7. Visualize a white light coming and encircling the main card.
8. Sit in silence and think about your intended outcome.
9. Take out a tarot card book and read the descriptions of the 5 cards that are encircling the main card. Does it give you any insight into your issue?
10. Thank the spiritual guardians of the tarot and release them.
11. For the next 10 days, carry the **Emperor** card with you wherever you go. Place it under your pillow at night. Every time you touch it, think of your intention.

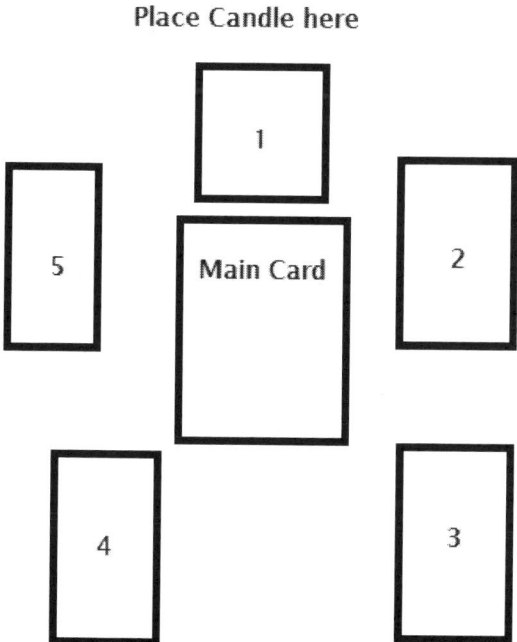

That concludes the ritual.

RITUAL 6 – THE HIEROPHANT: A RITUAL TO GAIN SPIRITUAL AND SACRED KNOWLEDGE

1. Place **the Hierophant card** at the center of the altar.
2. Pick up the card and think about the intention you have for this ritual.
3. Say the prayer to the spiritual guardians of the tarot. You may use your wording, this is just an example that I use.

   "Hear me Oh Great Guardians of the Tarot, harness me the power of this card, the card of hidden and mysterious wisdom. Hear me so that I may be endowed with the great mysteries of the universe. So Mote it me."
4. Place the card back in its spot.
5. From the same deck, randomly pull out 5 cards. Place those cards in such a way that they encircle the main card. As seen below.

6. Place the **violet and purple** candles right before the 1st card. As seen below. You can light and place the incense wherever you like. The incense is more for the ambience.
7. Visualize a white light coming and encircling the main card.
8. Sit in silence and think about your intended outcome.
9. Take out a tarot card book and read the descriptions of the 5 cards that are encircling the main card. Does it give you any insight into your issue?
10. Thank the spiritual guardians of the tarot and release them.
11. For the next 10 days, carry the **Hierophant** card with you wherever you go. Place it under your pillow at night. Every time you touch it, think of your intention.

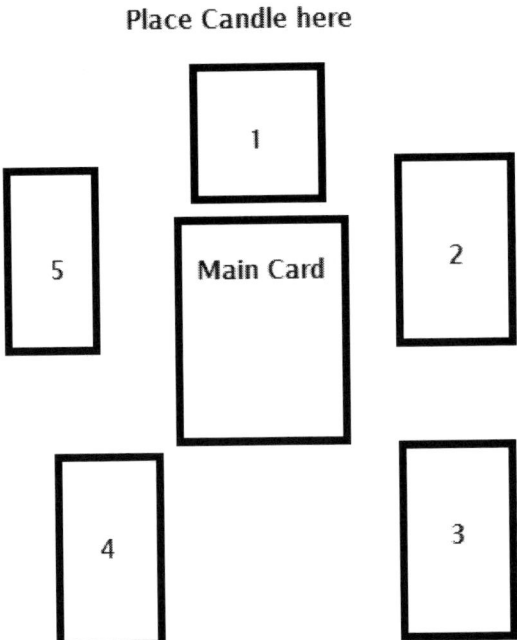

That concludes the ritual.

RITUAL 7 – THE LOVERS: A RITUAL TO ATTRACT A LOVING RELATIONSHIP

1. Place **the Lovers card** at the center of the altar.
2. Pick up the card and think about the intention you have for this ritual.
3. Say the prayer to the spiritual guardians of the tarot. You may use your wording, this is just an example that I use.
   "Hear me Oh Great Guardians of the Tarot, harness me the power of this card, the card of lovers. May the power of this great card attract to me the loving partner that is meant for me now. So Mote it me."
4. Place the card back in its spot.
5. From the same deck, randomly pull out 5 cards. Place those cards in such a way that they encircle the main card. As seen below.

6. Place the **Red and Pink** candles right before the 1st card. As seen below. You can light and place the incense wherever you like. The incense is more for the ambience.
7. Visualize a white light coming and encircling the main card.
8. Sit in silence and think about your intended outcome.
9. Take out a tarot card book and read the descriptions of the 5 cards that are encircling the main card. Does it give you any insight into your issue?
10. Thank the spiritual guardians of the tarot and release them.
11. For the next 10 days, carry the **Lovers** card with you wherever you go. Place it under your pillow at night. Every time you touch it, think of your intention.

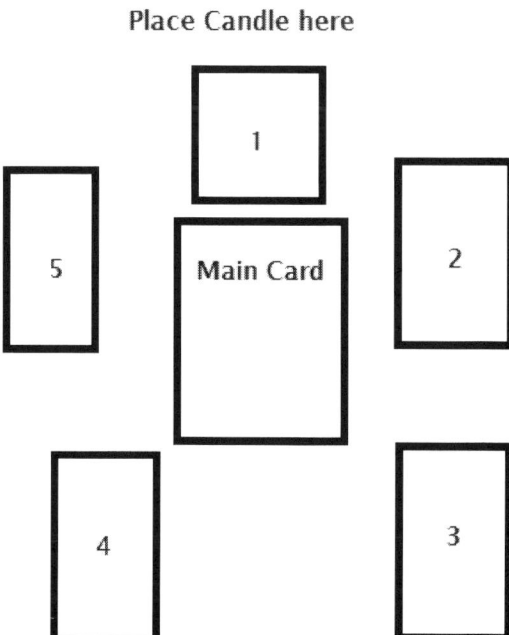

That concludes the ritual.

RITUAL 8 – THE CHARIOT: A RITUAL TO GAIN SELF CONFIDENCE

1. Place **the Chariot card** at the center of the altar.
2. Pick up the card and think about the intention you have for this ritual.
3. Say the prayer to the spiritual guardians of the tarot. You may use your wording, this is just an example that I use.

   "Hear me Oh Great Guardians of the Tarot, harness me the power of this card. May the energies of this card come to my aide. May I attract all that is needed for me to gain inner strength and self-confidence so I may walk through life with ease. So Mote it me."
4. Place the card back in its spot.

5. From the same deck, randomly pull out 5 cards. Place those cards in such a way that they encircle the main card. As seen below.
6. Place the **Orange and Yellow** candles right before the 1st card. As seen below. You can light and place the incense wherever you like. The incense is more for the ambience.
7. Visualize a white light coming and encircling the main card.
8. Sit in silence and think about your intended outcome.
9. Take out a tarot card book and read the descriptions of the 5 cards that are encircling the main card. Does it give you any insight into your issue?
10. Thank the spiritual guardians of the tarot and release them.
11. For the next 10 days, carry the **Chariot** card with you wherever you go. Place it under your pillow at night. Every time you touch it, think of your intention.

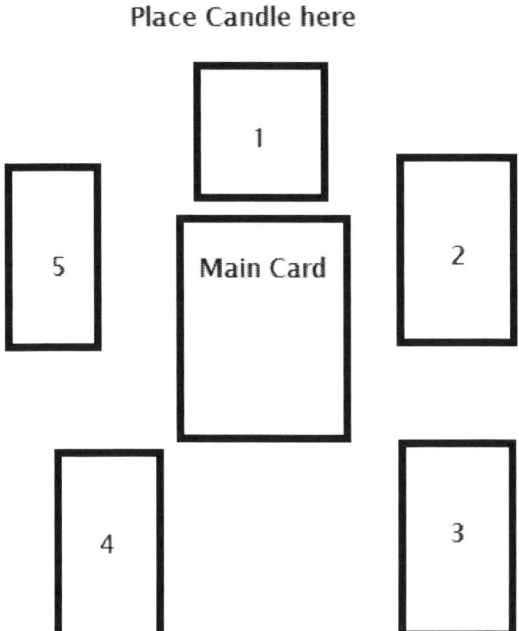

That concludes the ritual.

RITUAL 9 – THE STRENGTH CARD: A RITUAL TO STRENGTH IN THE FACE OF ADVERSITY

1. Place **the Strength card** at the center of the altar.
2. Pick up the card and think about the intention you have for this ritual.
3. Say the prayer to the spiritual guardians of the tarot. You may use your wording, this is just an example that I use.
   "Hear me Oh Great Guardians of the Tarot, harness me the power of this card. May I develop the strength and courage to withstand the current hardship in my life. By the grace of this card I will be strong. So Mote it me."
4. Place the card back in its spot.
5. From the same deck, randomly pull out 5 cards. Place those cards in such a way that they encircle the main card. As seen below.

6. Place the **black and white** candles right before the 1st card. As seen below. You can light and place the incense wherever you like. The incense is more for the ambience.
7. Visualize a white light coming and encircling the main card.
8. Sit in silence and think about your intended outcome.
9. Take out a tarot card book and read the descriptions of the 5 cards that are encircling the main card. Does it give you any insight into your issue?
10. Thank the spiritual guardians of the tarot and release them.
11. For the next 10 days, carry the **Strength** card with you wherever you go. Place it under your pillow at night. Every time you touch it, think of your intention.

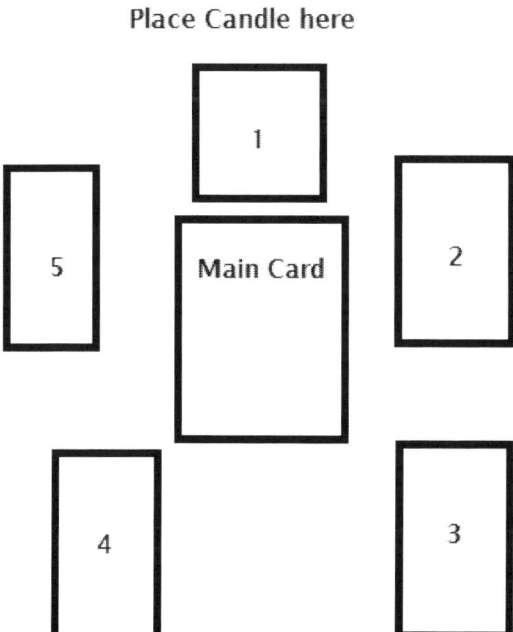

That concludes the ritual.

RITUAL 10 – THE HERMIT: A RITUAL TO ATTAIN INNER WISDOM AND MINDFULNESS

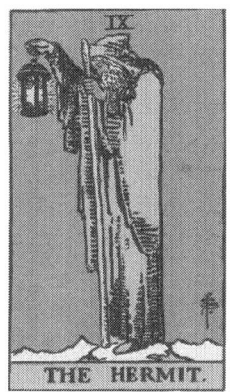

1. Place **the Hermit card** at the center of the altar.
2. Pick up the card and think about the intention you have for this ritual.
3. Say the prayer to the spiritual guardians of the tarot. You may use your wording, this is just an example that I use.

   "Hear me Oh Great Guardians of the Tarot, harness me the power of this card. May the powers vested in the Hermit pass on to me so that I may develop a rich inner life and gain mindfulness in the face of life on this earth. So Mote it me."
4. Place the card back in its spot.
5. From the same deck, randomly pull out 5 cards. Place those cards in such a way that they encircle the main card. As seen below.

6. Place the **Blue** and **white** candles right before the 1st card. As seen below. You can light and place the incense wherever you like. The incense is more for the ambience.
7. Visualize a white light coming and encircling the main card.
8. Sit in silence and think about your intended outcome.
9. Take out a tarot card book and read the descriptions of the 5 cards that are encircling the main card. Does it give you any insight into your issue?
10. Thank the spiritual guardians of the tarot and release them.
11. For the next 10 days, carry the **Hermit** card with you wherever you go. Place it under your pillow at night. Every time you touch it, think of your intention.

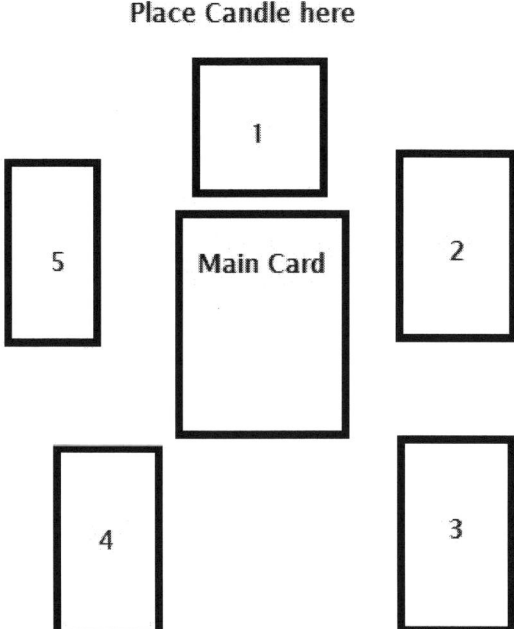

That concludes the ritual.

RITUAL 11 – THE WHEEL OF FORTUNE: A RITUAL TO ATTAIN THE ABILITY TO SEE THE BIGGER PICTURE

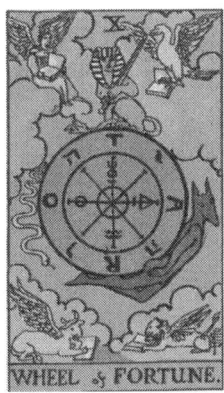

1. Place **the Wheel of Fortune card** at the center of the altar.
2. Pick up the card and think about the intention you have for this ritual.
3. Say the prayer to the spiritual guardians of the tarot. You may use your wording, this is just an example that I use.

   "Hear me Oh Great Guardians of the Tarot, harness me the power of this card. Often I am not able to see the divine reasoning behind events, by the power of this card, may I become aware of the divine lining behind all events in my life. So Mote it me."
4. Place the card back in its spot.

5. From the same deck, randomly pull out 5 cards. Place those cards in such a way that they encircle the main card. As seen below.
6. Place the **Green** and **white** candles right before the 1st card. As seen below. You can light and place the incense wherever you like. The incense is more for the ambience.
7. Visualize a white light coming and encircling the main card.
8. Sit in silence and think about your intended outcome.
9. Take out a tarot card book and read the descriptions of the 5 cards that are encircling the main card. Does it give you any insight into your issue?
10. Thank the spiritual guardians of the tarot and release them.
11. For the next 10 days, carry the **Wheel of Fortune** card with you wherever you go. Place it under your pillow at night. Every time you touch it, think of your intention.

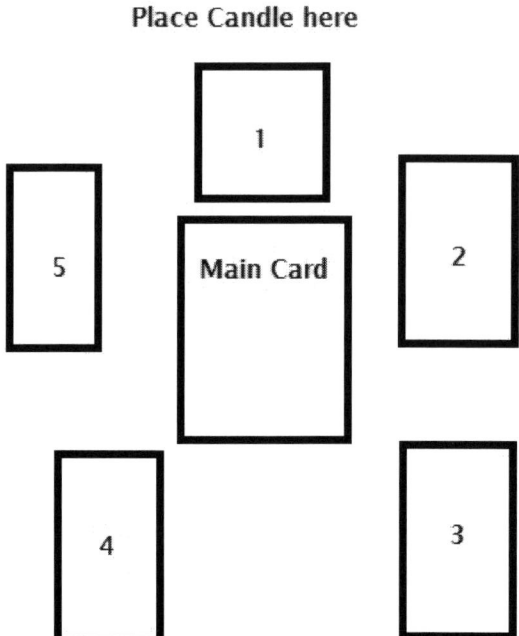

That concludes the ritual.

RITUAL 12 – THE JUSTICE CARD: A RITUAL TO GAIN INSTANT CLARITY ON ISSUES

1. Place **the Justice card** at the center of the altar.
2. Pick up the card and think about the intention you have for this ritual.
3. Say the prayer to the spiritual guardians of the tarot. You may use your wording, this is just an example that I use.
   "Hear me Oh Great Guardians of the Tarot, harness me the power of this card. Grant me the clarity I need regarding _____. So Mote it me."
4. Place the card back in its spot.
5. From the same deck, randomly pull out 5 cards. Place those cards in such a way that they encircle the main card. As seen below.

6. Place the **Blue** and **Purple** candles right before the 1st card. As seen below. You can light and place the incense wherever you like. The incense is more for the ambience.
7. Visualize a white light coming and encircling the main card.
8. Sit in silence and think about your intended outcome.
9. Take out a tarot card book and read the descriptions of the 5 cards that are encircling the main card. Does it give you any insight into your issue?
10. Thank the spiritual guardians of the tarot and release them.
11. For the next 10 days, carry the **Justice** card with you wherever you go. Place it under your pillow at night. Every time you touch it, think of your intention.

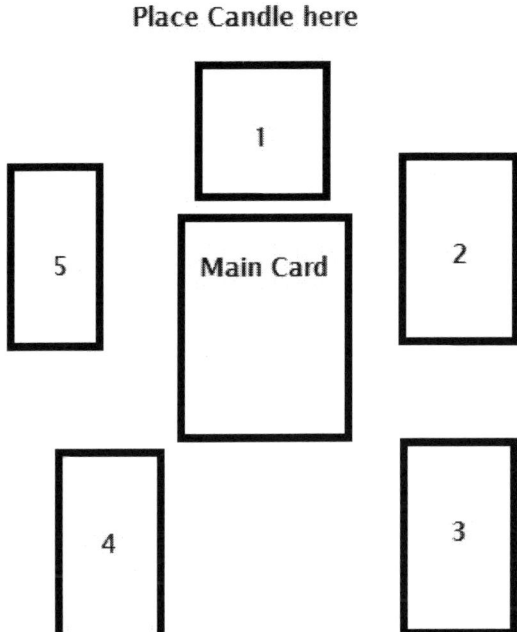

That concludes the ritual.

RITUAL 13 – THE HANGED MAN: A RITUAL TO OVERCOME TRAUMA

1. Place **the Hanged man card** at the center of the altar.
2. Pick up the card and think about the intention you have for this ritual.
3. Say the prayer to the spiritual guardians of the tarot. You may use your wording, this is just an example that I use.
   "Hear me Oh Great Guardians of the Tarot, harness me the power of this card. I have unresolved hurts in my life that I must get rid of. May the power of this card and by your power may I overcome this trauma of _____ So Mote it me."
4. Place the card back in its spot.

5. From the same deck, randomly pull out 5 cards. Place those cards in such a way that they encircle the main card. As seen below.
6. Place the **black** and **white** candles right before the 1st card. As seen below. You can light and place the incense wherever you like. The incense is more for the ambience.
7. Visualize a white light coming and encircling the main card.
8. Sit in silence and think about your intended outcome.
9. Take out a tarot card book and read the descriptions of the 5 cards that are encircling the main card. Does it give you any insight into your issue?
10. Thank the spiritual guardians of the tarot and release them.
11. For the next 10 days, carry the **Hanged man card** with you wherever you go. Place it under your pillow at night. Every time you touch it, think of your intention.

Place Candle here

| 1 |

| 5 | **Main Card** | 2 |

| 4 | | 3 |

That concludes the ritual.

RITUAL 14 – THE DEATH CARD: A RITUAL TO LET GO OF THE PAST

1. Place **the Death card** at the center of the altar.
2. Pick up the card and think about the intention you have for this ritual.
3. Say the prayer to the spiritual guardians of the tarot. You may use your wording, this is just an example that I use.

   "Hear me Oh Great Guardians of the Tarot, harness me the power of this card. There are issues in my life that I must overcome, by the power of this card, I request the ability to overcome this past event that has caused me harm. So Mote it me."
4. Place the card back in its spot.

5. From the same deck, randomly pull out 5 cards. Place those cards in such a way that they encircle the main card. As seen below.
6. Place the **black** and **white** candles right before the 1st card. As seen below. You can light and place the incense wherever you like. The incense is more for the ambience.
7. Visualize a white light coming and encircling the main card.
8. Sit in silence and think about your intended outcome.
9. Take out a tarot card book and read the descriptions of the 5 cards that are encircling the main card. Does it give you any insight into your issue?
10. Thank the spiritual guardians of the tarot and release them.
11. For the next 10 days, carry the **Death card** with you wherever you go. Place it under your pillow at night. Every time you touch it, think of your intention.

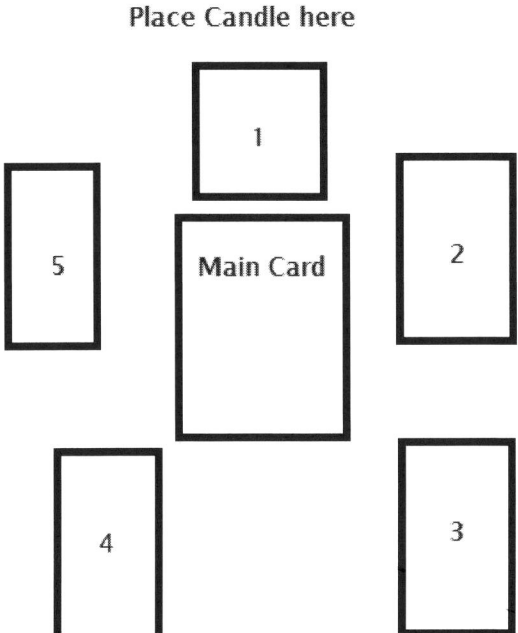

That concludes the ritual.

RITUAL 15 – THE TEMPERANCE CARD: A RITUAL TO RESOLVE INNER CONFLICTS

1. Place **the Temperance card** at the center of the altar.
2. Pick up the card and think about the intention you have for this ritual.
3. Say the prayer to the spiritual guardians of the tarot. You may use your wording, this is just an example that I use.
   "Hear me Oh Great Guardians of the Tarot, harness me the power of this card. I am divided within myself and I need to become whole. May the power of this card and your power bestow unity upon my. So Mote it me."
4. Place the card back in its spot.
5. From the same deck, randomly pull out 5 cards. Place those cards in such a way that they encircle the main card. As seen below.

6. Place the **blue** and **white** candles right before the 1st card. As seen below. You can light and place the incense wherever you like. The incense is more for the ambience.
7. Visualize a white light coming and encircling the main card.
8. Sit in silence and think about your intended outcome.
9. Take out a tarot card book and read the descriptions of the 5 cards that are encircling the main card. Does it give you any insight into your issue?
10. Thank the spiritual guardians of the tarot and release them.
11. For the next 10 days, carry the **Temperance card** with you wherever you go. Place it under your pillow at night. Every time you touch it, think of your intention.

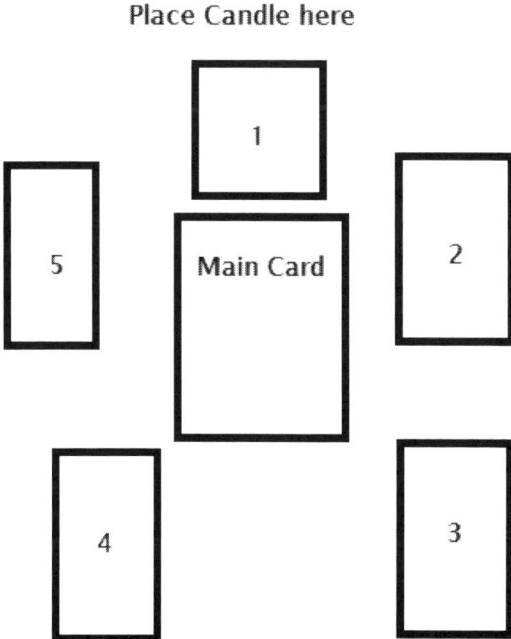

That concludes the ritual.

RITUAL 16 – THE DEVIL CARD: A RITUAL TO FREE ONESSELF FROM EMOTIONAL BONDAGE

1. Place **the Devil card** at the center of the altar.
2. Pick up the card and think about the intention you have for this ritual.
3. Say the prayer to the spiritual guardians of the tarot. You may use your wording, this is just an example that I use.

    "Hear me Oh Great Guardians of the Tarot, harness me the power of this card. I am in emotional bondage and I cannot release myself. I request by the power that is representative in this card that I be free of this bondage. So Mote it me."
4. Place the card back in its spot.

5. From the same deck, randomly pull out 5 cards. Place those cards in such a way that they encircle the main card. As seen below.
6. Place the **black** and **white** candles right before the 1st card. As seen below. You can light and place the incense wherever you like. The incense is more for the ambience.
7. Visualize a white light coming and encircling the main card.
8. Sit in silence and think about your intended outcome.
9. Take out a tarot card book and read the descriptions of the 5 cards that are encircling the main card. Does it give you any insight into your issue?
10. Thank the spiritual guardians of the tarot and release them.
11. For the next 10 days, carry the **Devil card** with you wherever you go. Place it under your pillow at night. Every time you touch it, think of your intention.

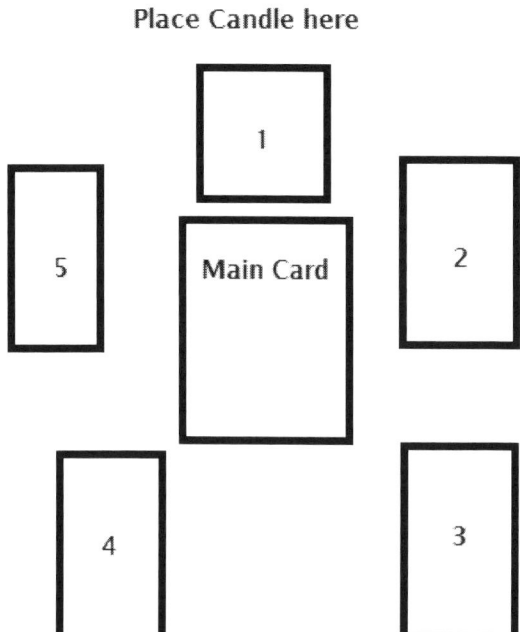

That concludes the ritual.

RITUAL 17 – THE TOWER CARD: A RITUAL TO FREE YOURSELF OF DESTRUCTIVE EGO

1. Place **the Tower card** at the center of the altar.
2. Pick up the card and think about the intention you have for this ritual.
3. Say the prayer to the spiritual guardians of the tarot. You may use your wording, this is just an example that I use.

   "Hear me Oh Great Guardians of the Tarot, harness me the power of this card. I am too full of ego and it does not allow me to understand others and makes me rigid in life. By the powers vested in this card, I ask to be humbled in a gentle way. So Mote it me."
4. Place the card back in its spot.

5. From the same deck, randomly pull out 5 cards. Place those cards in such a way that they encircle the main card. As seen below.
6. Place the **black** candles right before the 1st card. As seen below. You can light and place the incense wherever you like. The incense is more for the ambience.
7. Visualize a white light coming and encircling the main card.
8. Sit in silence and think about your intended outcome.
9. Take out a tarot card book and read the descriptions of the 5 cards that are encircling the main card. Does it give you any insight into your issue?
10. Thank the spiritual guardians of the tarot and release them.
11. For the next 10 days, carry the **Tower card** with you wherever you go. Place it under your pillow at night. Every time you touch it, think of your intention.

Place Candle here

```
         ┌─────┐
         │  1  │
         └─────┘
┌───┐   ┌─────────┐   ┌───┐
│ 5 │   │Main Card│   │ 2 │
└───┘   │         │   └───┘
        └─────────┘
   ┌───┐           ┌───┐
   │ 4 │           │ 3 │
   └───┘           └───┘
```

That concludes the ritual.

RITUAL 18 – THE STAR: A RITUAL TO DEVELOP FAITH IN LIFE

1. Place **the Star card** at the center of the altar.
2. Pick up the card and think about the intention you have for this ritual.
3. Say the prayer to the spiritual guardians of the tarot. You may use your wording, this is just an example that I use.

   "Hear me Oh Great Guardians of the Tarot, harness me the power of this card. Often I am pessimistic about life and do not have the faith to realize that all is working out as it should be. I ask that this card help me increase my faith. So Mote it me."
4. Place the card back in its spot.

5. From the same deck, randomly pull out 5 cards. Place those cards in such a way that they encircle the main card. As seen below.
6. Place the **pink and white** candles right before the 1st card. As seen below. You can light and place the incense wherever you like. The incense is more for the ambience.
7. Visualize a white light coming and encircling the main card.
8. Sit in silence and think about your intended outcome.
9. Take out a tarot card book and read the descriptions of the 5 cards that are encircling the main card. Does it give you any insight into your issue?
10. Thank the spiritual guardians of the tarot and release them.
11. For the next 10 days, carry the **Star card** with you wherever you go. Place it under your pillow at night. Every time you touch it, think of your intention.

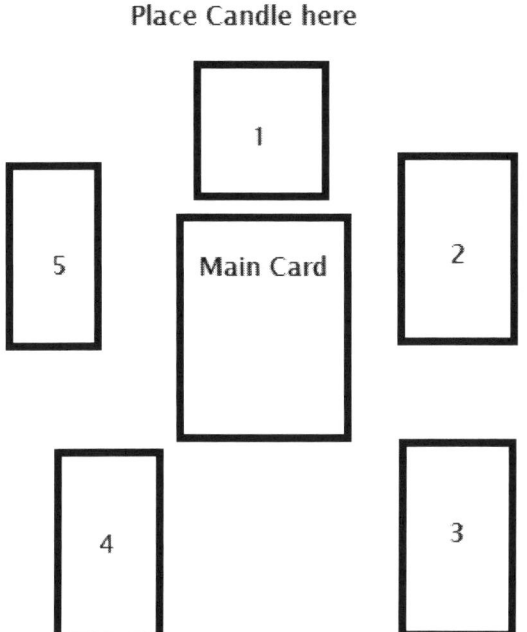

That concludes the ritual.

RITUAL 19 – THE MOON: A RITUAL TO MAKE YOU A MORE POWERFUL MAGICIAN

1. Place **the Moon card** at the center of the altar.
2. Pick up the card and think about the intention you have for this ritual.
3. Say the prayer to the spiritual guardians of the tarot. You may use your wording, this is just an example that I use.

   "Hear me Oh Great Guardians of the Tarot, harness me the power of this card. I ask that I be bestowed with enormous magickal powers, that all my rituals will be powerful and effective. So Mote it me."
4. Place the card back in its spot.
5. From the same deck, randomly pull out 5 cards. Place those cards in such a way that they encircle the main card. As seen below.

6. Place the **Violet** candles right before the 1st card. As seen below. You can light and place the incense wherever you like. The incense is more for the ambience.
7. Visualize a white light coming and encircling the main card.
8. Sit in silence and think about your intended outcome.
9. Take out a tarot card book and read the descriptions of the 5 cards that are encircling the main card. Does it give you any insight into your issue?
10. Thank the spiritual guardians of the tarot and release them.
11. For the next 10 days, carry the **Moon card** with you wherever you go. Place it under your pillow at night. Every time you touch it, think of your intention.

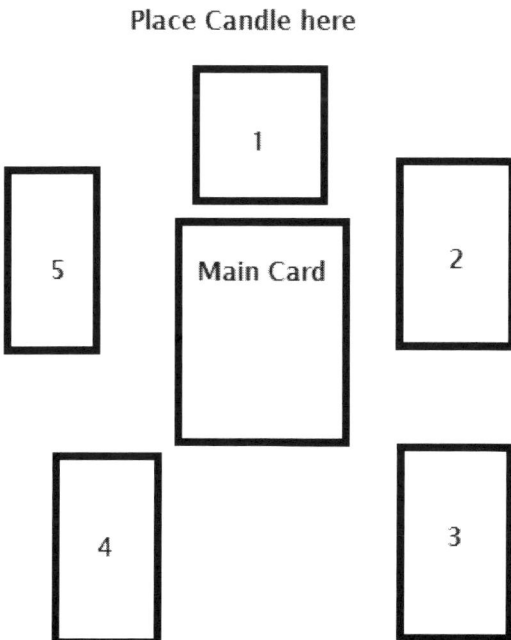

That concludes the ritual.

RITUAL 20 – THE SUN: A RITUAL TO MAKE ONESELF A SUCCESS AT ALL THINGS

1. Place **the Sun card** at the center of the altar.
2. Pick up the card and think about the intention you have for this ritual.
3. Say the prayer to the spiritual guardians of the tarot. You may use your wording, this is just an example that I use.

   "Hear me Oh Great Guardians of the Tarot, harness me the power of this card. I ask that I be bestowed with outstanding and boundless ability to succeed at all that I do. May I develop the Midas touch. So Mote it me."
4. Place the card back in its spot.

5. From the same deck, randomly pull out 5 cards. Place those cards in such a way that they encircle the main card. As seen below.
6. Place the **Orange and yellow** candles right before the 1st card. As seen below. You can light and place the incense wherever you like. The incense is more for the ambience.
7. Visualize a white light coming and encircling the main card.
8. Sit in silence and think about your intended outcome.
9. Take out a tarot card book and read the descriptions of the 5 cards that are encircling the main card. Does it give you any insight into your issue?
10. Thank the spiritual guardians of the tarot and release them.
11. For the next 10 days, carry the **Sun card** with you wherever you go. Place it under your pillow at night. Every time you touch it, think of your intention.

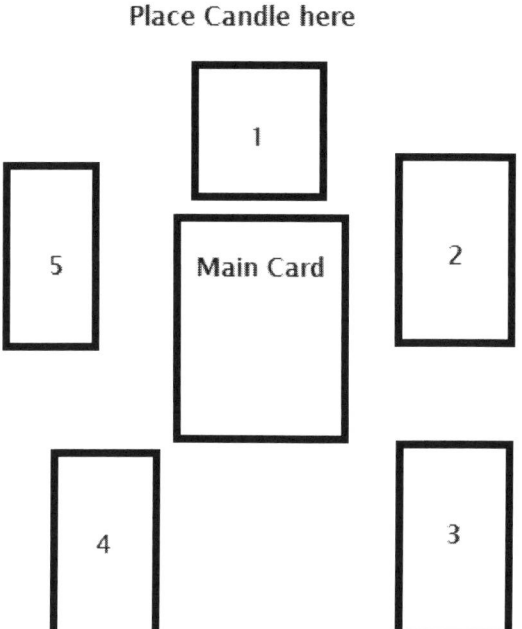

That concludes the ritual.

RITUAL 21 – THE JUDGEMENT CARD: A RITUAL TO MAKE LIFE MORE JOYFUL

1. Place **the Judgement card** at the center of the altar.
2. Pick up the card and think about the intention you have for this ritual.
3. Say the prayer to the spiritual guardians of the tarot. You may use your wording, this is just an example that I use.

   "Hear me Oh Great Guardians of the Tarot, harness me the power of this card. I ask that I be bestowed with purpose and joy in my life and that all my endeavors will be powerful and full of joy. So Mote it me."
4. Place the card back in its spot.
5. From the same deck, randomly pull out 5 cards. Place those cards in such a way that they encircle the main card. As seen below.

6. Place the **Orange, yellow and white** candles right before the 1st card. As seen below. You can light and place the incense wherever you like. The incense is more for the ambience.
7. Visualize a white light coming and encircling the main card.
8. Sit in silence and think about your intended outcome.
9. Take out a tarot card book and read the descriptions of the 5 cards that are encircling the main card. Does it give you any insight into your issue?
10. Thank the spiritual guardians of the tarot and release them.
11. For the next 10 days, carry the **Judgement card** with you wherever you go. Place it under your pillow at night. Every time you touch it, think of your intention.

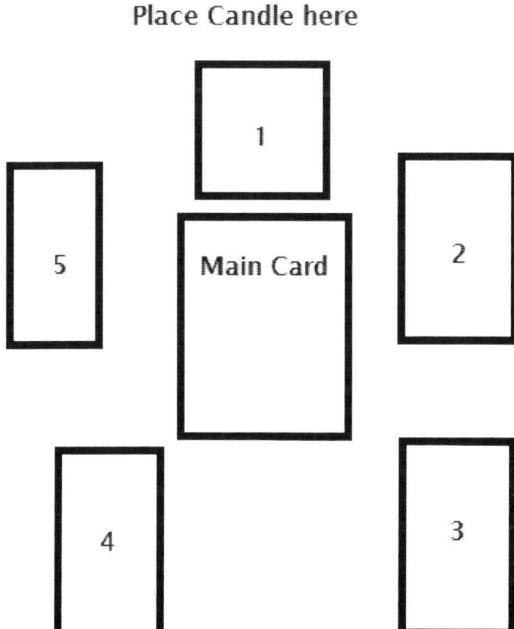

That concludes the ritual.

RITUAL 22 – THE WORLD: A RITUAL FOR THE ATTAINMENT OF ALL GOALS

1. Place **the World card** at the center of the altar.
2. Pick up the card and think about the intention you have for this ritual.
3. Say the prayer to the spiritual guardians of the tarot. You may use your wording, this is just an example that I use.
   "Hear me Oh Great Guardians of the Tarot, harness me the power of this card. I ask that I be bestowed with enormous powers of success and fulfillment and that all my days will be filled with purpose and success. So Mote it me."
4. Place the card back in its spot.
5. From the same deck, randomly pull out 5 cards. Place those cards in such a way that they encircle the main card. As seen below.

6. Place the **Yellow, Orange and Violet** candles right before the 1st card. As seen below. You can light and place the incense wherever you like. The incense is more for the ambience.
7. Visualize a white light coming and encircling the main card.
8. Sit in silence and think about your intended outcome.
9. Take out a tarot card book and read the descriptions of the 5 cards that are encircling the main card. Does it give you any insight into your issue?
10. Thank the spiritual guardians of the tarot and release them.
11. For the next 10 days, carry the **World card** with you wherever you go. Place it under your pillow at night. Every time you touch it, think of your intention.

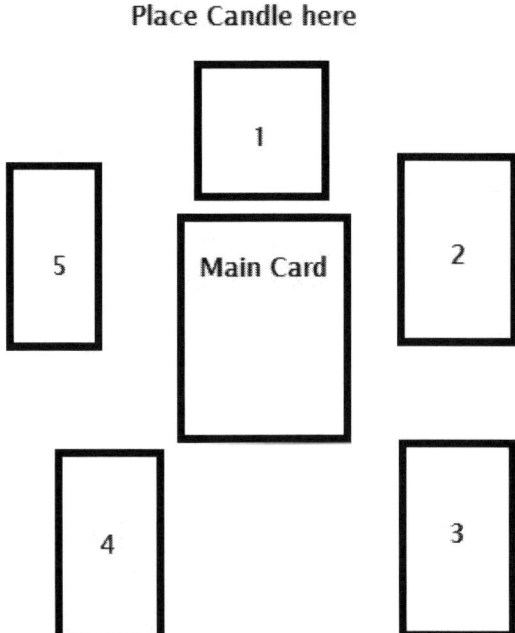

That concludes the ritual.

Conclusion

This concludes Tarot Magick. As you have seen, it is quite simple. You can do these rituals as often as you like. You can also do multiple rituals for the same issue and see what information you can glean. As you see, there is no pomp and circumstance, no expensive ritual garments and paraphernalia, no odd and impossible herbs to obtain, no directions to turn to, no contrived and pompous terminology and phrases to this kind of magick. Just magick , unconventional magick at that. I am filled with utmost confidence that once you have performed one or all these rituals, you will enter a magickal partnership with the Tarot like you never have before. You will find yourself using them over and over again. Although we used only the Major Arcana, feel free to use the lesser cards as well. May all your Magick be fruitful and effective.
And So It Is.

Other books by the author

The Mantra Magick Series:

VASHIKARAN MAGICK - LEARN THE DARK MANTRAS OF SUBJUGATION

Kali Mantra Magick: Summoning The Dark Powers of Kali Ma

Seed Mantra Magick: Master The Primordial Sounds of The universe

Chakra Mantra Magick: Tap Into The Magick Of Your Chakras

Tara Mantra Magick: How To Use The Power Of The Goddess Tara

Tibetan Mantra Magick: Tap Into The Power Of Tibetan Mantras

The Scared Names Series:

THE 72 NAMES OF GOD - THE 72 KEYS OF TRANSFORMATION

THE 72 ANGELS OF THE NAME - CALLING ON THE 72 ANGELS OF GOD

THE 99 NAMES OF ALLAH - ACQUIRING THE 99 DIVINE QUALITIES OF GOD

THE HIDDEN NAMES OF GENESIS - TAP INTO THE HIDDEN POWER OF MANIFESTATION

THE 72 DEMONS OF THE NAME - CALLING UPON THE GREAT DEMONS OF THE NAME

The 42 Letter Name of God: The Mystical Name Of Manifestation (Sacred Names Book 6)

Magick Of the Saints Series

Mary Magick: Calling Forth The Divine Mother For Help

The Magick of Saint Expedite: Tap Into the Truly Miraculous Power of Saint Expedite

Ouija Board Magic Series

OUIJA BOARD MAGICK - ARCHANGEL EDITION: COMMUNICATE AND HARNESS THE POWER OF THE GREAT ARCHANGELS

Crystal Magick Mantra Series

Moldavite Magick - Tap Into The Stone of Transformation

Supernatural Attainment Series

Tap Into The Power Of The Chant: Attaining Supernatural Abilities Using Mantras

Daemonic Magick

The Daemonic Companion: Creating Daemonic Entities To Do Your Will

Vedic Magick

Vedic Magick: Using Ancient Vedic Spells To Attain Wealth

Quantum Magick

The Quantum Magician – Enhancing Your Magick with a Parallel Life

Made in the USA
Middletown, DE
14 December 2016